FIDGET SPINNER
Ultimate Tricks
(50 ideas)

K Lancaster

Sphynx Publications

Fidget Spinner: Ultimate Tricks (50 Ideas)

ISBN: 978-0-244-30918-3

© K Lancaster 2017

10 9 8 7 6 5 4 3 2 1

Contents

About This Book

This book contains 50 fun ideas and tricks for you to try with your Fidget Spinners.

Towards the back of the book there is space for you to write four tricks of your own.

The ideas and tricks in this book are rated according to their difficulty and how dangerous they are. The easiest ideas are at the front of the book, and the tricks get increasingly difficult towards the end of the book.

Difficulty ratings
The tricks and ideas are rated 1 to 4 based on their level of difficulty:

1 = Easy

2 = Medium

3 = Difficult

4 = Extremely difficult

Danger ratings

The tricks and ideas are rated 1 to 4 based on the danger they pose:

1 = Not dangerous

2 = Slightly dangerous

3 = Moderately dangerous

4 = Dangerous

Any time a Fidget Spinner is thrown or released, there is a danger that it may hurt you or someone else, or that it may break something. Be extra cautious that the Fidget Spinner doesn't hit you in the eye!

At the back of the book is a checklist for you to tick off the ideas and tricks you have mastered.

Increasing the difficulty
Some of the tricks have suggestions for how you can increase the difficulty of the trick.

Many tricks can be made more difficult by doing one or more of the following:

- Use a light-up Fidget Spinner and do the trick in the dark

- Increase the number of Fidget Spinners you use

- Catch the Fidget Spinner on your fingertip rather than between your thumb and finger

- Join tricks together in a sequence (e.g. bounce it on your hand, then your knee, then your elbow)

Catching the Fidget Spinner
When catching the Fidget Spinner, you should catch the central bearing between your thumb and finger(s), unless the instructions tell you otherwise.

Remember that when catching the Fidget Spinner, the aim is for it to continue spinning after you've caught it.

Hole in One

Difficulty: 1   Danger: 2

You will need:

- 1 Fidget Spinner

Instructions:

1. Hold the Fidget Spinner in one hand between your thumb and finger

2. Spin the Fidget Spinner

3. With your other hand, make a circle with your thumb and first finger

4. Push your spinning Fidget Spinner into the circle on your other hand – the aim is to get one paddle of the Fidget Spinner neatly through the hole

Finger Spin

Difficulty: **1**   Danger: **1**

You will need:

- 1 Fidget Spinner

Instructions:

1. Hold the centre of the Fidget Spinner between your thumb and finger, with your thumb on top
2. Spin the Fidget Spinner
3. Remove your thumb, and balance the Fidget Spinner on your finger

Pencil Poke

Difficulty: **1**   Danger: **1**

You will need:

- 1 Fidget Spinner with holes in the paddles
- 1 pencil or pen

Instructions:

1. Hold the centre of the Fidget Spinner between your thumb and finger
2. Spin the Fidget Spinner
3. Hold a pen or pencil in the other hand
4. Poke the pen or pencil at the spinning Fidget Spinner – the aim is to get the end of the pen or pencil directly through the hole in the paddle

Roly Poly

Difficulty: 1   Danger: 2

You will need:

- 1 Fidget Spinner with holes in the paddles
- 50cm piece of string

Instructions:

1. Thread a piece of string through a hole in one of the paddles
2. Hold one end of the string in each hand so that the Fidget Spinner is in the middle
3. Roll your hands forwards in a circular motion so that the Fidget Spinner moves around in a circle
4. Increase the speed of your spinning

Pulsar

Difficulty: `1` Danger: `1`

You will need:

- 2 or more Fidget Spinners

Instructions:

1. Hold two Fidget Spinners between your thumb and finger
2. Spin one Fidget Spinner in one direction, and the other Fidget Spinner in the other direction

More difficult:

- Use three or more Fidget Spinners and spin them in alternating directions

Cog Machine

Difficulty: **1**   Danger: **1**

You will need:

- Several Fidget Spinners with three paddles

Instructions:

1. Place a Fidget Spinner on a flat surface

2. Place another Fidget Spinner next to the first, so that the paddle of one Fidget Spinner sits in the gap of the other Fidget Spinner

3. Continue to add other Fidget Spinners in the same way

4. Once assembled, turning one Fidget Spinner should turn all the others

Pencil Spinning Top

Difficulty: **1**   Danger: **1**

You will need:

- 1 Fidget Spinner with a hole in the central bearing
- 1 pencil
- 1 piece of paper

Instructions:

1. Insert the pencil through the centre hole of the Fidget Spinner, close to the pencil's lead
2. Spin the Fidget Spinner
3. Place the lead of the pencil onto the paper

More interesting:

Add one or more additional pencils into the holes on the paddles

Pen Tower

Difficulty: **1**   Danger: **1**

You will need:

- 2 tri Fidget Spinners with holes in the paddles
- 6 pens of equal length

Instructions:

1. Poke a pen through each hole on the Fidget Spinner
2. Stand it up so that the pens are upright, and the Fidget Spinner is at the top
3. Use another Fidget Spinner, and poke pens through its holes in the same way
4. Balance the second tower on top of the first

Hand Stack

Difficulty: 1   Danger: 1

You will need:

- 3 or more Fidget Spinners

Instructions:

1. Place one of the Fidget Spinners on the palm of your hand
2. Spin the Fidget Spinner
3. Place anther Fidget Spinner on top of the first, so that the central bearing balances on the first Fidget Spinner
4. Spin the Fidget Spinner
5. Continue adding as many Fidget Spinners as you can

More difficult:

Balance the Fidget Spinners on your fingertip

Stool Spin

Difficulty: 1   Danger: 1

You will need:

- 3-4 Fidget Spinners
- A chair or stool

Instructions:

1. Turn the chair or stool upside down (if it is a chair with a back, you will need to turn it upside down onto a table, with the back rest hanging off the edge of the table)

2. Balance a Fidget Spinner onto each leg of the chair or stool

3. Spin the Fidget Spinners

Floor Drop

Difficulty: ■ 1   Danger: ■ 1

You will need:

- 1 Fidget Spinner
- A hard floor (or table)

Instructions:

1. Hold one side of the central bearing of the Fidget Spinner between the nails of your thumb and finger(s)
2. Spin the Fidget Spinner
3. Drop the Fidget Spinner onto the floor
4. If dropped correctly, the Fidget Spinner should land on its central bearing and continue spinning

More difficult:

Drop the Fidget Spinner from a greater height

Forehead Balance

Difficulty: **1** Danger: **2**

You will need:

- 1 Fidget Spinner

Instructions:

1. Lie on your back on the floor
2. Place the Fidget Spinner on your forehead
3. Spin the Fidget Spinner

More difficult:

- Stack two or more Fidget Spinners on your forehead

Kneesie

Difficulty: **1**   Danger: **1**

You will need:

- 2 Fidget Spinners

Instructions:

1. Sit on the floor, with your knees bent upwards and your feet flat on the floor

2. Balance a Fidget Spinner on each knee

3. Spin the Fidget Spinners

Coin Stacker

Difficulty: **1**   Danger: **1**

You will need:

- 1 Fidget Spinner
- Several coins

Instructions:

1. Stack the coins on top of one another
2. Place the centre of the Fidget Spinner on top of the stack of coins
3. Spin the Fidget Spinner

More difficult:

- Use more coins in the stack

Nose Balance

Difficulty: 2   Danger: 2

You will need:

- 1 Fidget Spinner

Instructions:

1. Lie on your back, or tilt your head backwards while standing
2. Balance the Fidget Spinner on your nose
3. Spin the Fidget Spinner

Spinner Kiss

Difficulty: **2**　　　Danger: **2**

You will need:

- 1 Fidget Spinner

Instructions:

1. Lie on your back on the floor
2. Pucker up your lips, as if kissing or whistling
3. Balance the Fidget Spinner on your puckered lips
4. Spin the Fidget Spinner

Stigmata

Difficulty: 2   Danger: 1

You will need:

- 2 Fidget Spinners

Instructions:

1. Place one Fidget Spinner onto your wrist, with your palm facing upwards

2. Use your other hand to spin the Fidget Spinner

3. Stretch your arm out to your side

4. Stretch your other arm out to the other side, with your palm facing upwards

5. Spin a Fidget Spinner on your other wrist (you may need a friend to help you do this)

Air Hockey

Difficulty: **2**   Danger: **4**

You will need:

- 2 or more Fidget Spinners
- A clear table top

Instructions:

1. Place one or more Fidget Spinners at one side of the table
2. Spin the Fidget Spinners
3. Place another Fidget Spinner at the other side of the table
4. Spin the Fidget Spinner
5. Slide the Fidget Spinner across the table into the other Fidget Spinners

Thumbs Up

Difficulty: **2**   Danger: **2**

You will need:

- 2 Fidget Spinners

Instructions:

1. Hold one Fidget Spinner between your thumb and finger in one hand, with your thumb underneath

2. Do the same with the other Fidget Spinner in your other hand

3. Spin both Fidget Spinners

4. Remove your fingers so that both Fidget Spinners are balanced on your thumbs in the 'thumbs up' sign

Shoulder Spins

Difficulty: **2**   Danger: **1**

You will need:

- 2 Fidget Spinners

Instructions:

1. Place one Fidget Spinner onto each shoulder (if you have long hair, ensure it is tied back away from the Fidget Spinners)
2. Spin the Fidget Spinners

More difficult:

- Walk around with the Fidget Spinners spinning on your shoulders

Super Slow Stacker

Difficulty: **1**   Danger: **2**

You will need:

- 1 Fidget Spinner
- Coins or other small objects

Instructions:

1. Place the Fidget Spinner on a flat surface
2. Place a coin or other small object on each paddle
3. Begin spinning the Fidget Spinner slowly, then gradually increase its speed
4. Spin the Fidget Spinner as fast as you can without the coins falling off

Hand Twist

Difficulty: `2`   Danger: `1`

You will need:

- 1 Fidget Spinner

Instructions:

1. Hold the centre of the Fidget Spinner between your thumb and finger

2. Spin the Fidget Spinner

3. Move your elbow out to the side, and twist your hand underneath your elbow until your hand is pointing out to the side

4. Bring your whole arm around to your front and upwards

5. Continue moving your hand over your head and then over your shoulder

6. Move your hand around into its original position

Palm Catch

Difficulty: **2**   Danger: **2**

You will need:

- 1 Fidget Spinner

Instructions:

1. Hold the centre of the Fidget Spinner between your thumb and finger, with your thumb on top
2. Spin the Fidget Spinner
3. Gently throw the Fidget Spinner up into the air
4. Catch the Fidget Spinner on the palm of your hand

More difficult:

- Catch the Fidget Spinner on the palm of your other hand

Ball Spin

Difficulty: **2**   Danger: **1**

You will need:

- 1 Fidget Spinner
- 1 football

Instructions:

1. Balance the Fidget Spinner on top of the football
2. Spin the Fidget Spinner

Simple Release

Difficulty: **2**   Danger: **2**

You will need:

- 1 Fidget Spinner

Instructions:

1. Hold the centre of the Fidget Spinner between your thumb and finger
2. Spin the Fidget Spinner
3. Gently throw the Fidget Spinner up into the air
4. Catch the Fidget Spinner

Hand Bounce

Difficulty: **2**   Danger: **2**

You will need:

- 1 Fidget Spinner

Instructions:

1. Hold the centre of the Fidget Spinner between your thumb and finger
2. Spin the Fidget Spinner
3. Gently throw the Fidget Spinner up into the air
4. As the Fidget Spinner begins to fall, use the back of your hand to bounce it up again
5. Catch the Fidget Spinner

Elbow Bounce

Difficulty: 2   Danger: 2

You will need:

- 1 Fidget Spinner

Instructions:

1. Hold the centre of the Fidget Spinner between your thumb and finger
2. Spin the Fidget Spinner
3. Gently throw the Fidget Spinner up into the air
4. As the Fidget Spinner begins to fall, use your bent elbow to bounce it up again
5. Catch the Fidget Spinner

Flipper

Difficulty: **2**   Danger: **1**

You will need:

- 1 Fidget Spinner

Instructions:

1. Hold the centre of the Fidget Spinner between your thumb and finger, with your thumb on top and finger on the bottom
2. Spin the Fidget Spinner
3. Release the Fidget Spinner
4. Quickly turn over your hand
5. Catch the Fidget Spinner with your finger on top and your thumb on the bottom

Hand Transfer

Difficulty: `2`   Danger: `2`

You will need:

- 1 Fidget Spinner

Instructions:

1. Hold the centre of the Fidget Spinner between your thumb and finger
2. Spin the Fidget Spinner
3. Gently throw the Fidget Spinner up into the air
4. Catch the Fidget Spinner in your other hand

Balloon Bounce

Difficulty: **2**   Danger: **2**

You will need:

- 1 Fidget Spinner
- 1 balloon (inflated)

Instructions:

1. Place the inflated balloon on the floor, and wait until it is perfectly still
2. Hold the centre of the Fidget Spinner between your thumb and finger, about 50cm above the centre of the balloon
3. Spin the Fidget Spinner
4. Drop the Fidget Spinner onto the balloon. The Fidget Spinner should bounce upwards
5. Catch the Fidget Spinner

Clapper

Difficulty: 2   Danger: 2

You will need:

- 1 Fidget Spinner

Instructions:

1. Hold the centre of the Fidget Spinner between your thumb and finger
2. Spin the Fidget Spinner
3. Throw the Fidget Spinner fairly high into the air
4. Clap your hands
5. Catch the Fidget Spinner

Rulefilp

Difficulty: 2   Danger: 2

You will need:

- 1 Fidget Spinner
- 1 ruler

Instructions:

1. Hold the centre of the Fidget Spinner between your thumb and finger
2. Spin the Fidget Spinner
3. With your free hand, hold one end of the ruler
4. Balance the Fidget Spinner onto the free end of the ruler
5. Gently throw the Fidget Spinner up into the air
6. Catch the Fidget Spinner on the ruler

Walkies

Difficulty: **2**   Danger: **1**

You will need:

- 2 Fidget Spinners

Instructions:

1. Put on some shoes
2. Place a Fidget Spinner on the toes of each shoe
3. Spin the Fidget Spinners
4. Walk around with the Fidget Spinners balanced on your shoes

Knee Bounce

Difficulty: 2   Danger: 2

You will need:

- 1 Fidget Spinner

Instructions:

1. Hold the centre of the Fidget Spinner between your thumb and finger

2. Spin the Fidget Spinner

3. Gently throw the Fidget Spinner up into the air

4. As the Fidget Spinner begins to fall, use your knee to bounce it up again

5. Catch the Fidget Spinner

Finger Transfer

Difficulty: `3`   Danger: `1`

You will need:

- 1 Fidget Spinner

Instructions:

1. Hold the centre of the Fidget Spinner between your thumb and finger, with your thumb on top
2. Spin the Fidget Spinner
3. Remove your thumb and balance the Fidget Spinner on one finger
4. Gently throw the Fidget Spinner up 2cm
5. Catch the Fidget Spinner on a different finger

Pencil Catch

Difficulty: **3**   Danger: **2**

You will need:

- 1 Fidget Spinner with a hole in the central bearing
- 1 pencil or pen

Instructions:

1. Hold the pencil upright with the pointy end upwards
2. Place the Fidget Spinner onto the end of the pencil, so the point of the pencil pokes through the centre hole
3. Spin the Fidget Spinner
4. Gently throw the Fidget Spinner up into the air
5. Catch the Fidget Spinner on the end of the pencil

Hand Swap

Difficulty: **3**   Danger: **2**

You will need:

- 2 Fidget Spinners

Instructions:

1. Hold the centre of one Fidget Spinner between your thumb and finger
2. Hold the centre of the other Fidget Spinner between your thumb and finger in your other hand
3. Spin the Fidget Spinners
4. Gently throw both Fidget Spinners so that they cross over in the air
5. Catch the Fidget Spinners so that they have swapped hands

Kickstarter

Difficulty: **3**   Danger: **2**

You will need:

- 1 Fidget Spinner

Instructions:

1. Place the Fidget Spinner onto the top of your foot or shoe
2. Spin the Fidget Spinner
3. Kick the Fidget Spinner into the air
4. Catch the Fidget Spinner in your hand

Shoe Catch

Difficulty: **3**   Danger: **2**

You will need:

- 1 Fidget Spinner

Instructions:

1. Hold the centre of the Fidget Spinner between your thumb and finger
2. Spin the Fidget Spinner
3. Gently throw or drop the Fidget Spinner
4. Catch the Fidget Spinner on your shoe (wear shoes without laces, or tuck the laces away)

Arch

Difficulty: **3**   Danger: **3**

You will need:

- 1 Fidget Spinner

Instructions:

1. Hold the centre of the Fidget Spinner between your thumb and finger

2. Spin the Fidget Spinner

3. Hold both arms out to your sides at shoulder height

4. Throw the Fidget Spinner so that it arches over your head towards your other outstretched hand

5. Catch the Fidget Spinner in your other hand, with your arm outstretched

Person Transfer

Difficulty: **3**   Danger: **2**

You will need:

- 1 Fidget Spinner
- 1 friend

Instructions:

1. Hold the centre of the Fidget Spinner between your thumb and finger
2. Spin the Fidget Spinner
3. When your friend is ready, gently throw the Fidget Spinner to your friend
4. Your friend catches the Fidget Spinner

Around the Back

Difficulty: **4**　　　　Danger: **2**

You will need:

- 1 Fidget Spinner

Instructions:

1. Hold the centre of the Fidget Spinner between your thumb and finger
2. Spin the Fidget Spinner
3. Reach your hand around your back
4. Throw the Fidget Spinner forwards, and move your body to the side so that it doesn't hit you
5. Bring your hand quickly around to your front, and catch the Fidget Spinner

Person Swap

Difficulty: **4**   Danger: **3**

You will need:

- 2 Fidget Spinners
- 1 friend

Instructions:

1. Hold the centre of the Fidget Spinner between your thumb and finger
2. Spin the Fidget Spinner
3. Your friend should do the same with their Fidget Spinner
4. On the count of three, gently throw the Fidget Spinner to your friend, and your friend should throw theirs to you
5. Catch each other's Fidget Spinners

Plasma Bounce

Difficulty: **4**   Danger: **2**

You will need:

- 1 Fidget Spinner

Instructions:

1. Hold the centre of the Fidget Spinner between your thumb and finger
2. Spin the Fidget Spinner
3. Reach your hand around your back
4. Throw the Fidget Spinner forwards, and move your body to the side so that it doesn't hit you
5. As the Fidget Spinner begins to fall in front of you, use your knee to bounce it up again
6. Catch the Fidget Spinner

Somersault

Difficulty: 4   Danger: 2

You will need:

- 1 Fidget Spinner

Instructions:

1. Hold the centre of the Fidget Spinner between your thumb and finger
2. Spin the Fidget Spinner
3. Throw the Fidget Spinner up into the air, twisting your hand as you do so
4. The Fidget Spinner should rotate in the air
5. Catch the Fidget Spinner

Sunshine Switch

Difficulty: **4**   Danger: **2**

You will need:

- 1 Fidget Spinner

Instructions:

1. Hold the centre of the Fidget Spinner between your thumb and finger
2. Spin the Fidget Spinner
3. Lift one leg and reach your arm underneath it
4. Gently throw the Fidget Spinner up into the air
5. Quickly put your leg down, and lift your other leg
6. Quickly reach under your leg to catch the Fidget Spinner

Double Back

Difficulty: 4   Danger: 3

You will need:

- 1 Fidget Spinner

Instructions:

1. Hold the centre of the Fidget Spinner between your thumb and finger
2. Spin the Fidget Spinner
3. Reach your hand around your back
4. Gently throw the Fidget Spinner up into the air
5. Catch the Fidget Spinner in your other hand, behind your back

Back Catch

Difficulty: **4**   Danger: **3**

You will need:

- 1 Fidget Spinner

Instructions:

1. Hold the centre of the Fidget Spinner between your thumb and finger
2. Spin the Fidget Spinner
3. Throw the Fidget Spinner fairly high into the air
4. Bend over, and catch the Fidget Spinner on your back

Round You Go

Difficulty: **4**   Danger: **3**

You will need:

- 1 Fidget Spinner

Instructions:

1. Hold the centre of the Fidget Spinner between your thumb and finger
2. Spin the Fidget Spinner
3. Throw the Fidget Spinner high into the air
4. Spin around once
5. Catch the Fidget Spinner

Juggler

Difficulty: 4   **Danger:** 4

You will need:

- 3 or more Fidget Spinners

Instructions:

1. In one hand, hold one Fidget Spinner; in your other hand, hold the other two Fidget Spinners

2. Spin all of the Fidget Spinners

3. Juggle with the Fidget Spinners:

4. From the hand with two Fidget Spinners, throw one up into the air,

5. Follow this quickly by throwing the Fidget Spinner from your other hand

6. Throw the third Fidget Spinner

7. Keep throwing and catching Fidget Spinners so that you are juggling with them!

Trick name: ....

Difficulty: ☐   Danger: ☐

You will need:

- ... Fidget Spinner(s)

Instructions:

Trick name: ....

Difficulty: ☐   Danger: ☐

You will need:

- … Fidget Spinner(s)

Instructions:

Trick name: ....

Difficulty: ☐   Danger: ☐

You will need:

- … Fidget Spinner(s)

Instructions:

Trick name: ....

Difficulty: [ ]   Danger: [ ]

You will need:

- ... Fidget Spinner(s)

Instructions:

Trick Checklist

☐ Hole in One		☐ Hand Bounce	
☐ Finger Spin		☐ Elbow Bounce	
☐ Pencil Poke		☐ Flipper	
☐ Roly Poly		☐ Hand Transfer	
☐ Pulsar		☐ Balloon Bounce	
☐ Cog Machine		☐ Clapper	
☐ Pencil Spinning Top		☐ Ruleflip	
☐ Pen Tower		☐ Walkies	
☐ Hand Stack		☐ Knee Bounce	
☐ Stool Spin		☐ Finger Transfer	
☐ Floor Drop		☐ Pencil Catch	
☐ Forehead Balance		☐ Hand Swap	
☐ Kneesie		☐ Kickstarter	
☐ Coin Stacker		☐ Shoe Catch	
☐ Nose Balance		☐ Arch	
☐ Spinner Kiss		☐ Person Transfer	
☐ Stigmata		☐ Around the Back	
☐ Air Hockey		☐ Person Swap	
☐ Thumbs Up		☐ Plasma Bounce	
☐ Shoulder Spins		☐ Somersault	
☐ Super Slow Stacker		☐ Sunshine Switch	
☐ Hand Twist		☐ Double Back	
☐ Palm Catch		☐ Back Catch	
☐ Ball Spin		☐ Round You Go	
☐ Simple Release		☐ Juggler	

44733544R00039

Made in the USA
Middletown, DE
15 June 2017